MADLIBS®

FAMILY TREE MAD LIBS

By Roger Price and Leonard Stern

PSS!
PRICE STERN SLOAN

PRICE STERN SLOAN
Published by the Penguin Group
Penguin Group (USA) Inc., 375 Hudson Street, New York, New York 10014, USA
Penguin Group (Canada), 90 Eglinton Avenue East, Suite 700,
Toronto, Ontario, Canada M4P 2Y3
(a division of Pearson Penguin Canada Inc.)
Penguin Books Ltd, 80 Strand, London WC2R 0RL, England
Penguin Ireland, 25 St Stephen's Green, Dublin 2, Ireland (a division of Penguin Books Ltd)
Penguin Group (Australia), 250 Camberwell Road, Camberwell, Victoria 3124, Australia
(a division of Pearson Australia Group Pty Ltd)
Penguin Books India Pvt Ltd, 11 Community Centre,
Panchsheel Park, New Delhi–110 017, India
Penguin Group (NZ), 67 Apollo Drive, Mairangi Bay, Auckland 1311, New Zealand
(a division of Pearson New Zealand Ltd)
Penguin Books (South Africa) (Pty) Ltd, 24 Sturdee Avenue,
Rosebank, Johannesburg 2196, South Africa

Penguin Books Ltd, Registered Offices:
80 Strand, London WC2R 0RL, England

Published by Price Stern Sloan,
a division of Penguin Young Readers Group,
345 Hudson Street, New York, New York 10014.

ISBN 978-0-8431-1643-4

15 16

MAD LIBS
INSTRUCTIONS

MAD LIBS® is a game for people who don't like games!
It can be played by one, two, three, four, or forty.

• RIDICULOUSLY SIMPLE DIRECTIONS

In this tablet you will find stories containing blank spaces where words
are left out. One player, the READER, selects one of these stories. The
READER does not tell anyone what the story is about. Instead, he/she asks
the other players, the WRITERS, to give him/her words. These words are
used to fill in the blank spaces in the story.

• TO PLAY

The READER asks each WRITER in turn to call out a word—an adjective or
a noun or whatever the space calls for—and uses them to fill in the blank
spaces in the story. The result is a MAD LIBS® game.

When the READER then reads the completed MAD LIBS® game to the other
players, they will discover that they have written a story that is fantastic,
screamingly funny, shocking, silly, crazy, or just plain dumb—depending
upon which words each WRITER called out.

• EXAMPLE (*Before* and *After*)

"_____!" he said _____
    EXCLAMATION   ADVERB

as he jumped into his convertible _____ and
                                         NOUN

drove off with his _____ wife.
                       ADJECTIVE

"*Ouch!*_____!" he said *Stupidly*_____
    EXCLAMATION   ADVERB

as he jumped into his convertible *Cat* and
                                     NOUN

drove off with his *brave* wife.
                       ADJECTIVE

In case you have forgotten what adjectives, adverbs, nouns, and verbs are, here is a quick review:

An ADJECTIVE describes something or somebody. Lumpy, soft, ugly, messy, and short are adjectives.

An ADVERB tells how something is done. It modifies a verb and usually ends in "ly." Modestly, stupidly, greedily, and carefully are adverbs.

A NOUN is the name of a person, place, or thing. Sidewalk, umbrella, bridle, bathtub, and nose are nouns.

A VERB is an action word. Run, pitch, jump, and swim are verbs. Put the verbs in past tense if the directions say PAST TENSE. Ran, pitched, jumped, and swam are verbs in the past tense.

When we ask for A PLACE, we mean any sort of place: a country or city (Spain, Cleveland) or a room (bathroom, kitchen).

An EXCLAMATION or SILLY WORD is any sort of funny sound, gasp, grunt, or outcry, like Wow!, Ouch!, Whomp!, Ick!, and Gadzooks!

When we ask for specific words, like a NUMBER, a COLOR, an ANIMAL, or a PART OF THE BODY, we mean a word that is one of those things, like seven, blue, horse, or head.

When we ask for a PLURAL, it means more than one. For example, cat pluralized is cats.

MAD LIBS® is fun to play with friends, but you can also play it by yourself! To begin with, DO NOT look at the story on the page below. Fill in the blanks on this page with the words called for. Then, using the words you have selected, fill in the blank spaces in the story.

Now you've created your own hilarious MAD LIBS® game!

NO RUSH TO RUSHMORE

NOUN _____

PART OF THE BODY _____

NOUN _____

ADJECTIVE _____

PART OF THE BODY _____

NOUN _____

ADJECTIVE _____

ADJECTIVE _____

NOUN _____

NUMBER _____

ADJECTIVE _____

NOUN _____

NOUN _____

PLURAL NOUN _____

MAD LIBS

DINING ROOM WARS

Our dining _____ used to be a war _____.
               NOUN   NOUN

I thought the battles about correct table _____ would
                                                PLURAL NOUN

never end. It was us kids versus Mom, and it seemed like a fight

that would last to the _____ end. But tonight Dad finally
                                ADJECTIVE

declared a/an _____ truce, and we negotiated a/an
                        ADJECTIVE

_____ peace _____. Mom promised to no
  ADJECTIVE   NOUN

longer get _____ upset and shoot us dirty _____
              ADVERB   PLURAL NOUN

and make _____ remarks when we do _____
           ADJECTIVE   ADJECTIVE

things she doesn't like. We in turn agreed to:

    1) Use napkins to wipe our _____ and not
                                       PART OF THE BODY (PLURAL)

our _____.
    PLURAL NOUN

    2) Keep our _____ off the table.
                  PART OF THE BODY (PLURAL)

    3) Not use our _____ to pick up _____
                    PART OF THE BODY (PLURAL)   PLURAL NOUN

from our plates—except for sandwiches or pieces of

_____.
    NOUN

    4) Never talk with food in our _____.
                              PART OF THE BODY (PLURAL)

From FAMILY TREE MAD LIBS® • Copyright © 2007 by Price Stern Sloan, a division of
Penguin Young Readers Group, 345 Hudson Street, New York, NY 10014.

MAD LIBS® is fun to play with friends, but you can also play it by yourself! To begin with, DO NOT look at the story on the page below. Fill in the blanks on this page with the words called for. Then, using the words you have selected, fill in the blank spaces in the story.

Now you've created your own hilarious MAD LIBS® game!

OUR FAVORITE UNCLE

NOUN _____

ADJECTIVE _____

PART OF THE BODY _____

ADJECTIVE _____

ADJECTIVE _____

NUMBER _____

PLURAL NOUN _____

NOUN _____

PART OF THE BODY _____

NUMBER _____

PLURAL NOUN _____

NOUN _____

NOUN _____

NOUN _____

PART OF THE BODY _____

NOUN _____

PLURAL NOUN _____

ADJECTIVE _____

ADJECTIVE _____

ADJECTIVE _____

MAD LIBS®

OUR FAVORITE UNCLE

Every kid has a favorite aunt or _____. The mere
                                    NOUN

mention of Uncle Sid's name brings a/an _____ smile
                                              ADJECTIVE

to the _____ of everyone in our _____
         PART OF THE BODY   ADJECTIVE

family. In size he resembles a/an _____ mountain,
                                        ADJECTIVE

being _____ feet tall and weighing two hundred and
           NUMBER

forty _____. He's so strong, he can lift a grand
         PLURAL NOUN

_____ with one _____ and bench-press
     NOUN   PART OF THE BODY

_____ _____ without working up a/an
     NUMBER   PLURAL NOUN

_____. And he can do it as gracefully as a ballet
     NOUN

_____. Generous and warm, he has a heart of
     NOUN

_____ and would give you the shirt off his _____
     NOUN   PART OF THE BODY

if you asked. Uncle Sid is a scientist who works around the

_____ to keep our water and _____ from
     NOUN   PLURAL NOUN

becoming polluted by _____ substances, and he does
                          ADJECTIVE

all of this with a/an _____ sense of humor. He's one
                          ADJECTIVE

_____ guy!
     ADJECTIVE

From FAMILY TREE MAD LIBS® • Copyright © 2007 by Price Stern Sloan, a division of
Penguin Young Readers Group, 345 Hudson Street, New York, NY 10014.

MAD LIBS® is fun to play with friends, but you can also play it by yourself! To begin with, DO NOT look at the story on the page below. Fill in the blanks on this page with the words called for. Then, using the words you have selected, fill in the blank spaces in the story.

Now you've created your own hilarious MAD LIBS® game!

FAREWELL ADDRESS TO OUR CAMPING TRIP

PART OF THE BODY _____

NOUN _____

NUMBER _____

PLURAL NOUN _____

ADJECTIVE _____

NOUN _____

PLURAL NOUN _____

NOUN _____

NOUN _____

PLURAL NOUN _____

NOUN _____

NOUN _____

PLURAL NOUN _____

PLURAL NOUN _____

PART OF THE BODY (PLURAL) _____

VERB ENDING IN "ING" _____

FAREWELL ADDRESS TO OUR CAMPING TRIP

Everyone in this family needs to have his or her _____

PART OF THE BODY

examined. Why are we going on another camping trip? Am I the

only one who remembers last year? On our way to the camp

_____, we had not one but _____ flat

NOUN   NUMBER

_____. Then, after we pitched our tent, a/an

PLURAL NOUN

_____ grizzly _____ trashed it, tore it into

ADJECTIVE   NOUN

little _____, and stared at us as he ate every morsel

PLURAL NOUN

of our first night's _____. We got by without our tent by

NOUN

building a roaring _____ and sleeping in the open air

NOUN

under a blanket of twinkling _____. But no sooner had

PLURAL NOUN

we fallen asleep than there was a sudden bolt of _____

NOUN

and a clap of _____, and it started raining cats and

NOUN

_____. By the time morning came we were wet and

PLURAL NOUN

loaded with mosquito _____ on our _____.

PLURAL NOUN   PART OF THE BODY (PLURAL)

Okay, now that I've refreshed your memory, do you still want to go

_____? You do? Go ahead . . . see if I care. Wait, I'm coming.

VERB ENDING IN "ING"

From FAMILY TREE MAD LIBS® • Copyright © 2007 by Price Stern Sloan, a division of
Penguin Young Readers Group, 345 Hudson Street, New York, NY 10014.

MAD LIBS® is fun to play with friends, but you can also play it by yourself! To begin with, DO NOT look at the story on the page below. Fill in the blanks on this page with the words called for. Then, using the words you have selected, fill in the blank spaces in the story.

Now you've created your own hilarious MAD LIBS® game!

TAKE ME OUT TO THE BALLGAME

NOUN _____

NOUN _____

NOUN _____

NOUN _____

PLURAL NOUN _____

PLURAL NOUN _____

ADJECTIVE _____

SILLY WORD _____

NOUN _____

PLURAL NOUN _____

NOUN _____

NOUN _____

NOUN _____

PLURAL NOUN _____

NOUN _____

NOUN _____

NOUN _____

VERB (PAST TENSE) _____

MAD LIBS®
TAKE ME OUT
TO THE BALLGAME

It's always great to attend a baseball _____, but it's an
                                        NOUN

extra special _____ to go with our grandfather. He's
                  NOUN

been a permanent _____ at the park since he was
                      NOUN

just a wee _____. Everyone there knows him, including
                NOUN

the _____ who sell hot, roasted _____ and
        PLURAL NOUN   PLURAL NOUN

even the _____ umpires. They all greet him with "Hiya,
              ADJECTIVE

_____," which was Grandpa's nickname when he was
    SILLY WORD

a little _____. We all thought that Grandpa's season
              NOUN

_____, located behind home _____,
    PLURAL NOUN   NOUN

were the best in the ballpark until our family was invited to sit in

the owners' _____ to celebrate Grandpa's 75th birthday.
                  NOUN

It was so exciting! As the organist played "Happy _____
                                                        NOUN

to You" and fifty thousand _____ sang along, Grandpa
                                PLURAL NOUN

was escorted to the pitcher's _____ to throw out the
                                  NOUN

first _____. Everyone in the _____-park
          NOUN   NOUN

_____, but our family was by far the loudest.
    VERB (PAST TENSE)

From FAMILY TREE MAD LIBS® • Copyright © 2007 by Price Stern Sloan, a division of
Penguin Young Readers Group, 345 Hudson Street, New York, NY 10014.

MAD LIBS® is fun to play with friends, but you can also play it by yourself! To begin with, DO NOT look at the story on the page below. Fill in the blanks on this page with the words called for. Then, using the words you have selected, fill in the blank spaces in the story.

Now you've created your own hilarious MAD LIBS® game!

ROOMING WITH SHAKESPEARE

ADJECTIVE _____

NOUN _____

NOUN _____

ADJECTIVE _____

NOUN _____

NOUN _____

NOUN _____

VERB _____

PLURAL NOUN _____

PLURAL NOUN _____

VERB ENDING IN "ING" _____

ADJECTIVE _____

NOUN _____

NOUN _____

ADJECTIVE _____

PLURAL NOUN _____

MAD LIBS®
ROOMING WITH SHAKESPEARE

My sister is a/an _____ pain in the _____. Last
                    ADJECTIVE   NOUN

year, when she tried out for the cheerleading _____, I
                                                      NOUN

never got a/an _____ night's sleep. Every five minutes I
                  ADJECTIVE

would hear, "Go, _____, go!" But as bad as that was, it's
                       NOUN

nothing compared to the _____ she's putting me through
                              NOUN

now. She was cast in the school's Shakespeare _____ and
                                                      NOUN

has become impossible to _____ with. She's so full of
                                VERB

herself—she carries her nose so high, it wipes the spider-_____
                                                        PLURAL NOUN

off the ceiling, and, if you can believe it, she answers her cell phone

with, "What sayest thou?" Yesterday she asked our dad to pay for

voice _____. For what? She has a non-_____
         PLURAL NOUN   VERB ENDING IN "ING"

part—she just carries a/an _____ _____
                              ADJECTIVE   NOUN

across the stage. Even if she drops it, all she can say is, "Oops."

But what's really driving me up the _____ is that she
                                          NOUN

and her _____ friends no longer "hang out"—now
              ADJECTIVE

they have afternoon tea and _____. What sayest thou?
                                  PLURAL NOUN

From FAMILY TREE MAD LIBS® • Copyright © 2007 by Price Stern Sloan, a division of
Penguin Young Readers Group, 345 Hudson Street, New York, NY 10014.

MAD LIBS® is fun to play with friends, but you can also play it by yourself! To begin with, DO NOT look at the story on the page below. Fill in the blanks on this page with the words called for. Then, using the words you have selected, fill in the blank spaces in the story.

Now you've created your own hilarious MAD LIBS® game!

HOME VIDEOS

ADJECTIVE _____

NOUN _____

ADJECTIVE _____

ADJECTIVE _____

ADVERB _____

NOUN _____

PART OF THE BODY _____

PART OF THE BODY (PLURAL) _____

PLURAL NOUN _____

ADVERB _____

PLURAL NOUN _____

PLURAL NOUN _____

NOUN _____

NOUN _____

PART OF THE BODY _____

NOUN _____

NUMBER _____

HOME VIDEOS

I did it again! Last night we had a/an _____ dinner
ADJECTIVE

to celebrate Mom and Dad's 17th wedding _____
NOUN

and later watch videos of their _____ courtship and
ADJECTIVE

_____ ceremony. As everyone in the family anticipated,
ADJECTIVE

I became _____ emotional. The moment Dad got down
ADVERB

on one _____ and asked Mom for her _____
NOUN PART OF THE BODY

in marriage, my _____ began to tremble and I burst
PART OF THE BODY (PLURAL)

into _____. Okay, I admit it, I'm _____
PLURAL NOUN ADVERB

sentimental, but the way Mom and Dad looked into each

other's _____ when they exchanged their wedding
PLURAL NOUN

_____ was a total _____-jerker. They're a
PLURAL NOUN NOUN

match made in _____. When the lights came on, there
NOUN

wasn't a dry _____ in the _____, and I had
PART OF THE BODY NOUN

personally gone through _____ packs of tissues.
NUMBER

MAD LIBS® is fun to play with friends, but you can also play it by yourself! To begin with, DO NOT look at the story on the page below. Fill in the blanks on this page with the words called for. Then, using the words you have selected, fill in the blank spaces in the story.

Now you've created your own hilarious MAD LIBS® game!

A VISIT TO THE ATTIC

NOUN _____

ADJECTIVE _____

NOUN _____

PART OF THE BODY (PLURAL) _____

ADVERB _____

NOUN _____

PLURAL NOUN _____

VERB _____

NOUN _____

NOUN _____

NOUN _____

ADVERB _____

NOUN _____

NOUN _____

NOUN _____

NOUN _____

MAD LIBS®

A VISIT TO THE ATTIC

On my last visit to the attic, I hit the jack-_____ when
                                               NOUN
I found an old letter Grandma had written to an advice columnist:

For the past three years I've had a great friendship with a/an

_____ _____. He's a good person
    ADJECTIVE   NOUN
and has both _____ planted _____
            PART OF THE BODY (PLURAL)   ADVERB
on the _____. We have many _____
            NOUN   PLURAL NOUN
in common. We both love to read, and we have the same taste

in music—like rock 'n' _____ and western, and
                          VERB
occasionally we go to hear a symphony _____ play.
                                          NOUN
Last night, he asked for my _____ in marriage. I
                               NOUN
was thrown for a/an _____. I've always thought
                        NOUN
of him as my friend. What to do?

Signed, _____ Anxious
         ADVERB
Dear Anxious: Marry the _____. Remember, a bird
                            NOUN
in the _____ is worth two in the _____.
            NOUN   NOUN
Thankfully, Grandma listened—that _____ she's
                                      NOUN
describing? That's my grandpa!

From FAMILY TREE MAD LIBS® • Copyright © 2007 by Price Stern Sloan, a division of
Penguin Young Readers Group, 345 Hudson Street, New York, NY 10014.

MAD LIBS® is fun to play with friends, but you can also play it by yourself! To begin with, DO NOT look at the story on the page below. Fill in the blanks on this page with the words called for. Then, using the words you have selected, fill in the blank spaces in the story.

Now you've created your own hilarious MAD LIBS® game!

DOUBLE FAULT

ADJECTIVE _____

PART OF THE BODY _____

PLURAL NOUN_____

PERSON IN ROOM (FEMALE) _____

PERSON IN ROOM (FEMALE) _____

NOUN _____

NOUN _____

PLURAL NOUN _____

PART OF THE BODY _____

NUMBER _____

PART OF THE BODY (PLURAL) _____

PLURAL NOUN _____

NOUN _____

NUMBER _____

ADJECTIVE _____

ADJECTIVE _____

VERB ENDING IN "ING"_____

PART OF THE BODY _____

MAD LIBS®

DOUBLE FAULT

It's embarrassing that in a family of _____ athletes,
ADJECTIVE

I'm the only one without any hand-_____ coordination.
PART OF THE BODY

So I asked my two _____, _____
PLURAL NOUN   PERSON IN ROOM (FEMALE)

and _____, for help. They're both on the varsity
PERSON IN ROOM (FEMALE)

_____ team. I didn't have the slightest _____
NOUN   NOUN

of what I was getting into. My two sweet _____ became
PLURAL NOUN

unbelievable trainers. They had me doing daily push-ups, sit-ups, and

deep _____ bends, and I was running _____
PART OF THE BODY   NUMBER

miles a day to strengthen my _____. I also had to do
PART OF THE BODY (PLURAL)

a series of deep-breathing _____ designed to improve
PLURAL NOUN

my _____ capacity. It was a grueling _____
NOUN   NUMBER

months before my _____ sisters deemed me ready for
ADJECTIVE

the _____ moment. Unfortunately, it never happened.
ADJECTIVE

As I was _____ at tryouts, I tripped and broke my
VERB ENDING IN "ING"

_____. Anyone up for chess?
PART OF THE BODY

MAD LIBS® is fun to play with friends, but you can also play it by yourself! To begin with, DO NOT look at the story on the page below. Fill in the blanks on this page with the words called for. Then, using the words you have selected, fill in the blank spaces in the story.

Now you've created your own hilarious MAD LIBS® game!

A STAND-UP UNCLE

NOUN _____

ADJECTIVE _____

NOUN _____

ADJECTIVE _____

PART OF THE BODY (PLURAL) _____

ADJECTIVE _____

ADJECTIVE _____

PLURAL NOUN _____

PLURAL NOUN _____

PLURAL NOUN _____

NOUN _____

ADJECTIVE _____

ADJECTIVE _____

ADJECTIVE _____

PART OF THE BODY _____

MAD LIBS®

A STAND-UP UNCLE

Every _____ in our _____ family believes
        NOUN   ADJECTIVE

Uncle George could be a stand-up _____. Like all
                                        NOUN

_____ comedians, Uncle George thinks fast on his
    ADJECTIVE

_____, and he has a really _____ delivery
PART OF THE BODY (PLURAL)   ADJECTIVE

and incredibly _____ timing. Five _____
              ADJECTIVE   PLURAL NOUN

after arriving at a party, he has the guests doubled over in laughter

with _____ running down their _____.
      PLURAL NOUN   PLURAL NOUN

They have to struggle to catch their _____. The
                                    NOUN

only people who might not laugh at his _____
                                  ADJECTIVE

jokes are his patients. Yes, patients! You see, Uncle George is

a dentist, and he tests his _____ new material on
                        ADJECTIVE

his patients while he works on their teeth. He has what most

_____ comics would give their right _____
  ADJECTIVE   PART OF THE BODY

for . . . a captive audience!

MAD LIBS® is fun to play with friends, but you can also play it by yourself! To begin with, DO NOT look at the story on the page below. Fill in the blanks on this page with the words called for. Then, using the words you have selected, fill in the blank spaces in the story.

Now you've created your own hilarious MAD LIBS® game!

PORTRAIT OF GREAT-GRANDMA

NOUN _____

NOUN _____

ADJECTIVE _____

NOUN _____

NOUN _____

NOUN _____

ADJECTIVE _____

PLURAL NOUN _____

PART OF THE BODY (PLURAL) _____

ADJECTIVE _____

PLURAL NOUN _____

PLURAL NOUN _____

ADJECTIVE _____

NOUN _____

ADJECTIVE _____

MAD LIBS®
PORTRAIT OF
GREAT-GRANDMA

A striking painting of Great-Grandma as a young _____
                                                      NOUN
has been hanging in our living _____ for as long as I can
                                      NOUN
remember. A local art dealer believes it was painted by James McNeill

Whistler, whose most _____ work is the painting of his
                          ADJECTIVE
_____ sitting in a rocking _____. It could be
      NOUN   NOUN
true. After all, Great-Grandma was the reigning _____
                                                      NOUN
of her day. With her _____ complexion, high cheek-
                          ADJECTIVE
_____, and vivid green _____, there
  PLURAL NOUN   PART OF THE BODY (PLURAL)
wasn't a portrait artist alive who didn't want to paint her. And she

had no end of _____ suitors. Over the years she was
                    ADJECTIVE
courted by crowned _____ of Europe as well as the
                          PLURAL NOUN
leading _____ of American society. I've often
              PLURAL NOUN
wondered why she married Great-Grandpa, because to tell the truth,

he was kind of _____-looking. When I asked Dad about
                    ADJECTIVE
it, he said Great-Grandpa was the only _____ who
                                              NOUN
could make her laugh. Isn't love _____?!
                                      ADJECTIVE

MAD LIBS® is fun to play with friends, but you can also play it by yourself! To begin with, DO NOT look at the story on the page below. Fill in the blanks on this page with the words called for. Then, using the words you have selected, fill in the blank spaces in the story.

Now you've created your own hilarious MAD LIBS® game!

COUSINS CLUB

PLURAL NOUN _____

NOUN _____

ADJECTIVE _____

NOUN _____

ADJECTIVE _____

CELEBRITY (FEMALE) _____

ADVERB _____

ADJECTIVE _____

ADVERB _____

ADJECTIVE _____

ADVERB _____

NOUN _____

VERB _____

NOUN _____

NOUN _____

VERB ENDING IN "ING" _____

ADVERB _____

ADJECTIVE _____

NOUN _____

SAME CELEBRITY _____

PLURAL NOUN _____

PLURAL NOUN _____

MAD LIBS®

COUSINS CLUB

It's amazing how alike some family _____ can be!
                                    PLURAL NOUN

When our _____ Club gets together every once in a/an
              NOUN

_____ _____, I'm reminded of how much one
    ADJECTIVE   NOUN

of my _____ cousins, _____, looks
            ADJECTIVE   CELEBRITY (FEMALE)

_____ like me. She even has _____
    ADVERB   ADJECTIVE

mannerisms that are _____ like mine. In fact, it's kind of
                            ADVERB

_____ how _____ similar we are. We're like
    ADJECTIVE   ADVERB

two peas in a/an _____. She likes to _____
                        NOUN   VERB

in class and do her home-_____ in the middle of
                                  NOUN

the _____, just like I do. And when it comes to
          NOUN

_____, her taste in boys is _____
VERB ENDING IN "ING"   ADVERB

like mine: tall, dark, and _____, with a great
                                  ADJECTIVE

sense of _____. I hope Cousin _____ and
              NOUN   SAME CELEBRITY

I will be close _____ for the rest of our _____.
                  PLURAL NOUN   PLURAL NOUN

From FAMILY TREE MAD LIBS® • Copyright © 2007 by Price Stern Sloan, a division of
Penguin Young Readers Group, 345 Hudson Street, New York, NY 10014.

MAD LIBS® is fun to play with friends, but you can also play it by yourself! To begin with, DO NOT look at the story on the page below. Fill in the blanks on this page with the words called for. Then, using the words you have selected, fill in the blank spaces in the story.

Now you've created your own hilarious MAD LIBS® game!

OUR FAVORITE RESTAURANT

NOUN _____

NOUN _____

ADJECTIVE _____

NOUN _____

NOUN _____

PLURAL NOUN _____

PLURAL NOUN _____

NOUN _____

ADJECTIVE _____

PLURAL NOUN _____

PLURAL NOUN _____

PLURAL NOUN _____

NOUN _____

NOUN _____

ADJECTIVE _____

NOUN _____

ADJECTIVE _____

NOUN _____

MAD LIBS®

OUR FAVORITE RESTAURANT

Our family's favorite eating _____ is the Shanghai

NOUN

_____. Dad loves it because it's a/an _____

NOUN   ADJECTIVE

walk from our house and he doesn't have to drive the

_____ guzzler. We love it because the Chinese food is out

NOUN

of this _____. We always order the same _____—

NOUN   PLURAL NOUN

steamed _____, minced _____ in lettuce

PLURAL NOUN   NOUN

cups, sweet-and-_____ barbecued _____, and

ADJECTIVE   PLURAL NOUN

a bowl of fried _____. Then comes the best part of

PLURAL NOUN

the meal—fortune _____! I always save my fortunes.

PLURAL NOUN

My current favorites are: 1) You will receive an important

_____ from a mysterious _____. 2) As the sun

NOUN   NOUN

rises, a/an _____ opportunity will present itself . . . be

ADJECTIVE

sure to take advantage of it before the _____ goes down.

NOUN

3) Tomorrow you will be called upon to make a/an _____

ADJECTIVE

decision that will affect the rest of your _____.

NOUN

From FAMILY TREE MAD LIBS® • Copyright © 2007 by Price Stern Sloan, a division of
Penguin Young Readers Group, 345 Hudson Street, New York, NY 10014.

MAD LIBS® is fun to play with friends, but you can also play it by yourself! To begin with, DO NOT look at the story on the page below. Fill in the blanks on this page with the words called for. Then, using the words you have selected, fill in the blank spaces in the story.

Now you've created your own hilarious MAD LIBS® game!

THE CASE OF THE MISSING TREE HOUSE

ADJECTIVE _____

NUMBER _____

NOUN _____

NOUN _____

NOUN _____

NOUN _____

ADJECTIVE _____

NOUN _____

NOUN _____

PLURAL NOUN _____

NOUN _____

PLURAL NOUN _____

NOUN _____

PART OF THE BODY (PLURAL) _____

VERB _____

NOUN _____

PART OF THE BODY (PLURAL) _____

PART OF THE BODY _____

NOUN _____

VERB _____

MAD☺LIBS®
THE CASE OF THE
MISSING TREE HOUSE

One of Dad's _____ childhood memories is of the
ADJECTIVE

_____-year-old oak _____ that his parents
NUMBER   NOUN

planted in the back-_____ of their first _____.
                              NOUN   NOUN

The tree was their pride and _____, and when I came along,
                                          NOUN

Grandpa built a/an _____ tree house in it. As our family
                              ADJECTIVE

grew, both the oak _____ and the tree _____
                              NOUN   NOUN

were used by me and my close _____. In fact, we named it
                                          PLURAL NOUN

"The Oak _____ Boys Club." No _____ were allowed.
                  NOUN   PLURAL NOUN

Then one morning, we awoke and found the tree _____
                                                                        NOUN

gone. No one could believe their _____.
                                              PART OF THE BODY (PLURAL)

A tree house doesn't just get up and _____ away. My dad
                                                      VERB

felt foolish having to file a Missing Tree House _____—
                                                                  NOUN

especially when he knew in his heart of _____that
                                                      PART OF THE BODY (PLURAL)

the splinter he'd pulled out of my sister's _____ that
                                                            PART OF THE BODY

morning was a direct link to the missing _____ house. If
                                                            NOUN

only the tree could _____, the mystery would be solved.
                              VERB

MAD LIBS® is fun to play with friends, but you can also play it by yourself! To begin with, DO NOT look at the story on the page below. Fill in the blanks on this page with the words called for. Then, using the words you have selected, fill in the blank spaces in the story.

Now you've created your own hilarious MAD LIBS® game!

FAMOUS ANCESTOR

NOUN _____

ADJECTIVE _____

PERSON IN ROOM (MALE) _____

PART OF THE BODY _____

ADJECTIVE _____

ADJECTIVE _____

NOUN _____

NOUN _____

PART OF THE BODY _____

VERB (PAST TENSE) _____

NOUN _____

PART OF THE BODY _____

NOUN _____

NOUN _____

NOUN _____

When Aunt Rose was a little _____, she won a/an

NOUN

_____ contest reciting a/an _____ and

NOUN · NOUN

singing her _____ version of "Yankee _____

ADJECTIVE · SILLY WORD

Dandy." From that moment on she was bitten by the acting

_____. Whenever and wherever there was a casting

NOUN

_____, Aunt Rose would show up and audition for the

NOUN

_____. Like all actors, she was turned down many, many

OCCUPATION

times, but to her credit it never dampened her _____.

PLURAL NOUN

She took rejection with a grain of _____ and always

NOUN

held her _____ up high. But when she had her first

PART OF THE BODY

child, to the family's surprise, she threw in the _____

NOUN

and became a stay-at-home _____. Now whenever Aunt

NOUN

Rose has the urge to perform, she sits at the piano and sings all the

old _____ songs for her grandchildren, nieces, and

ADJECTIVE

_____.

PLURAL NOUN

MAD LIBS® is fun to play with friends, but you can also play it by yourself! To begin with, DO NOT look at the story on the page below. Fill in the blanks on this page with the words called for. Then, using the words you have selected, fill in the blank spaces in the story.

Now you've created your own hilarious MAD LIBS® game!

THE GARAGE BAND

ADJECTIVE _____

ADJECTIVE _____

VERB _____

NOUN _____

VERB ENDING IN "ING" _____

NOUN _____

ADJECTIVE _____

PLURAL NOUN _____

ADJECTIVE _____

NOUN _____

SILLY WORD _____

PLURAL NOUN _____

ADJECTIVE _____

ADJECTIVE _____

PERSON IN ROOM _____

PERSON IN ROOM _____

PERSON IN ROOM _____

PLURAL NOUN _____

NOUN _____

NOUN _____

MAD LIBS®

THE GARAGE BAND

Dad plays a/an _____ piano. A/An _____
                    ADJECTIVE   ADJECTIVE

musician, he's equally at home with rock 'n' _____
                                                        VERB

as he is with classical _____. Mom has a remarkable
                              NOUN

_____ voice and was the lead _____ in
VERB ENDING IN "ING"   NOUN

her college choir. She never failed to hit a/an _____ note.
                                                      ADJECTIVE

Music flows through our family's _____—with the
                                        PLURAL NOUN

exception of Cousin Joel, who doesn't have a/an _____
                                                        ADJECTIVE

ear for music and can't carry a/an _____. But believe
                                          NOUN

it or not, he just formed a garage band. They are called the

_____ _____. Fortunately, Joel's only the
   SILLY WORD   PLURAL NOUN

_____ manager. Three of our other cousins make
   ADJECTIVE

up the _____ band. _____ plays guitar,
            ADJECTIVE   PERSON IN ROOM

_____ plays bass, and _____ plays the
PERSON IN ROOM   PERSON IN ROOM

_____. It's been only three weeks since they got
PLURAL NOUN

together and they've already been booked—at the local police

_____ for disturbing the _____.
   NOUN   NOUN

MAD LIBS® is fun to play with friends, but you can also play it by yourself! To begin with, DO NOT look at the story on the page below. Fill in the blanks on this page with the words called for. Then, using the words you have selected, fill in the blank spaces in the story.

Now you've created your own hilarious MAD LIBS® game!

PONDERING IN THE POUND

NOUN _____

PART OF THE BODY (PLURAL) _____

ADJECTIVE _____

ADJECTIVE _____

PLURAL NOUN _____

PLURAL NOUN _____

ADJECTIVE _____

ADJECTIVE _____

ADJECTIVE _____

ADJECTIVE _____

ADJECTIVE _____

PLURAL NOUN _____

NOUN _____

PLURAL NOUN _____

ADJECTIVE _____

Some of my fondest _____ from my _____
                   PLURAL NOUN   ADJECTIVE

childhood are of my father teaching my siblings and me to play

_____-ball, foot-_____, and other
      NOUN   NOUN

_____sports. He never said we'd end up in the Super
  ADJECTIVE

_____ or the World _____, but he did
     NOUN   NOUN

teach us to put our _____ and soul into the game and
                 PART OF THE BODY

play to the best of our _____. "It isn't whether you
                  PLURAL NOUN

win or _____," he would say, "but how you play the
        VERB

_____." He bought us a volley-_____ and
    NOUN   NOUN

put up a/an _____ net in our back-_____,
          ADJECTIVE   NOUN

and he also taught us how to play tennis on the public courts

near our _____. We were so lucky to have a/an
          NOUN

_____ family that did so many _____
   ADJECTIVE   ADJECTIVE

things together. Like they always say, the _____ that
                                       NOUN

plays together, stays together!

MAD LIBS® is fun to play with friends, but you can also play it by yourself! To begin with, DO NOT look at the story on the page below. Fill in the blanks on this page with the words called for. Then, using the words you have selected, fill in the blank spaces in the story.

Now you've created your own hilarious MAD LIBS® game!

CAR TRIP TRAVAILS

ADJECTIVE _____

PLURAL NOUN _____

NOUN _____

ADJECTIVE _____

ADJECTIVE _____

PART OF THE BODY (PLURAL) _____

NOUN _____

NOUN _____

NUMBER _____

PERSON IN ROOM (MALE) _____

PERSON IN ROOM (FEMALE) _____

PLURAL NOUN _____

ADJECTIVE _____

ADJECTIVE _____

PART OF THE BODY (PLURAL) _____

NOUN _____

NOUN _____

NOUN _____

MAD LIBS

CAR TRIP TRAVAILS

Based on many _____ past experiences, this family
                    ADJECTIVE

should never take car _____—certainly not together.
                        PLURAL NOUN

The last time the seven of us were all in one _____, there
                                              NOUN

were three _____ arguments, a/an _____
           ADJECTIVE   ADJECTIVE

fistfight, and a couple of bloody _____—and that was
                                  PART OF THE BODY (PLURAL)

just on the drive to the local super-_____. Recently, we
                                      NOUN

were on our way to Grandma and Grandpa's _____, which
                                          NOUN

is at least a/an _____-hour drive away. Dad was pulling out
                 NUMBER

of the driveway when my brother _____ and sister
                                PERSON IN ROOM (MALE)

_____ started to argue about who would read the
PERSON IN ROOM (FEMALE)

Mad _____ and who would fill in the _____
      PLURAL NOUN   ADJECTIVE

blanks. Dad brought the car to a/an _____ stop. He was so
                                    ADJECTIVE

angry, smoke seemed to be coming out of his _____.
                                            PART OF THE BODY (PLURAL)

"One more _____ out of any of you and this _____
          NOUN   NOUN

is over," he snapped. "Now, any questions?" Our kid brother timidly

raised his _____ and asked, "Are we there yet?"
           NOUN

This book is published by

PSS!

PRICE STERN SLOAN

whose other splendid titles include such literary classics as

The Original #1 Mad Libs®

Son of Mad Libs®

Sooper Dooper Mad Libs®

Monster Mad Libs®

Goofy Mad Libs®

Off-the-Wall Mad Libs®

Vacation Fun Mad Libs®

Camp Daze Mad Libs®

Christmas Fun Mad Libs®

Dinosaur Mad Libs®

Mad Libs® 40th Anniversary Deluxe Edition

Mad Mad Mad Mad Mad Libs®

Mad Libs® On the Road

The Apprentice™ Mad Libs®

The Powerpuff Girls™ Mad Libs®

Scooby-Doo!™ Mad Libs®

Flushed Away™ Mad Libs®

Happy Feet™ Mad Libs®

Madagascar™ Mad Libs®

Over the Hedge™ Mad Libs®

Operation™ Mad Libs®

SpongeBob SquarePants™ Mad Libs®

Fear Factor™ Mad Libs®

Fear Factor™ Mad Libs®: Ultimate Gross Out!

Survivor™ Mad Libs®

Guinness World Records™ Mad Libs®

Betty and Veronica® Mad Libs®

Napoleon Dynamite™ Mad Libs®

Nancy Drew® Mad Libs®

The Mad Libs® Worst-Case Scenario™ Survival Handbook

The Mad Libs® Worst-Case Scenario™ Survival Handbook 2

and many, many more!

Mad Libs® are available wherever books are sold